WHITE MOUSE
Nancy Wake
Robyn P. Watts

16

KNOWLEDGE
BOOKS AND SOFTWARE

© Knowledge Books and Software

Teacher Notes:

Nancy Wake's role in the French Resistance is inspiring to all Australians. She was incredibly brave, fearless and clever in avoiding capture by the Gestapo. Her contribution and bravery is a role model for young women and for all fair-minded people.

Discussion points for consideration:

1. What was the French Resistance and why did Nancy want to join?

2. Discuss the many attributes that Nancy demonstrated during her life, eg bravery, resilience, persistence, determination, leadership, goal-setting, problem-solving skills. What others can you think of?

3. Nancy was a true and selfless heroine who always put others before herself. Discuss how this would have been for a woman during these times and how she managed to succeed in her mission.

Difficult words to be introduced and practised before reading this book: Resistance, underground, Gestapo, journalist, inheritance, interview, connections, refugees, unidentified, desperate, communicate, leadership, installations, executed, headquarters, international, heroine, recommended, contribution, commitment, outstanding, sacrifices, servicewomen, independent, resourceful.

Contents

1. Who Is the White Mouse?
2. World War Two
3. The Resistance
4. What Was Nancy Doing in France?
5. France Becomes Nancy's Home
6. The French Resistance
7. The White Mouse
8. Did the Germans Find the White Mouse?
9. The War Ends

1. Who Is the White Mouse?

Nancy Wake was from Australia. She was born in New Zealand. She lived in Australia from the age of two. Why is Nancy Wake known as the *White Mouse*?

Nancy was a spy in France during World War Two. Germany had control over most of France. A lot of people resisted the Germans taking over their country.

Nancy played such an important role in World War Two she was nicknamed, the *White Mouse* by the German secret police! They were called the Gestapo.

2. World War Two

The German army overran the French army. The French army had to accept defeat. The war between Germany and France was over by June, 1940. Germany was in control of France. The German army was now all over France. The French people were very upset with German control. The Germans were brutal to anyone that tried to stop them.

If you were trying to resist, you would be shot, or sent to prison. A lot of people started resisting. This was called the Resistance. The Resistance was French people and people from overseas helping to stop the Germans. Nancy joined the Resistance.

3. The Resistance

Nancy Wake joined the French Resistance after World War Two started in 1939. Her job at the beginning of the war was to act as a smuggler. She would carry messages and food to underground Resistance fighters who were fighting the Germans who had invaded France.

The Gestapo put Nancy on their most wanted list. They named her *White Mouse* for the way she kept away from their traps. She was never caught.

Many others were caught and shot. It was very scary work as you never knew if you were going to be caught. Even this boy was shot.

The Resistance fighter's job was to slow the German army. This could be done by cutting phone wires, blowing up roads, bridges and train lines. Sending information back to England was important. Pilots and crew escaping Germany were helped to get back to England. Escaping prisoners of war were helped back to England.

The Resistance fighters were in small groups across France. They were not an army but people wanting to free their country again. Nancy joined the Resistance to fight Germany.

8

She was named the *White Mouse* because she was like a white mouse.

How does a white mouse behave?

A white mouse gets away before being caught. The mouse is very careful before moving. They sniff and listen carefully. Mice move fast and they eat quickly. A mouse will move out of reach when you try and pick them up with your hand.

This is a story of a very young Australian who faced being shot every day. Why did she want to fight the Germans? Nancy was very brave. The Germans were very careful in finding the Resistance fighters. Many of these brave people died.

4. What Was Nancy Doing in France?

Why would an Australian girl join the French resistance to fight the Germans? To better understand Nancy Wake, let's understand her background. Nancy lived in Australia from the age of two. Nancy was born in New Zealand.

She had a difficult time when she was young. Nancy's family lived in Sydney. Her mother was very strict and her father was a writer. Nancy's father left Nancy and her mother and went to live in New Zealand. He wanted to make a film about Maoris. He sold the family home and never came back. Nancy and her mother were evicted from their home.

Nancy and her mother had to find a home to rent. Nancy went to the local high school, and left school at the age of 16. She trained to become a nurse. She enjoyed nursing in Sydney. She saved her money and decided she wanted to train and work as a journalist. She used the savings from her nursing job and a small inheritance, and she decided to travel to London.

While in London, she trained and worked as a journalist. She enjoyed studying French at her Sydney high school and decided to visit France. She enjoyed visiting France so much that she decided to get a job as a journalist there.

5. France Becomes Nancy's Home

In France she met and married a rich factory owner named Henri Fiocca. Henry Fiocca and Nancy Wake lived in France. She was now able to do many things as she had the money to travel, buy stuff, and have a good time. Nancy was sensible and did not want to waste her time.

One of her early writing jobs in France was to interview Adolf Hitler. She had the job to write a story about him in a French newspaper. Can you imagine having this job to write a story about Hitler? She later spent all her effort trying to get rid of the Nazis. She really did know who she was fighting.

On holidays with her husband in 1939, Nancy visited Vienna in Austria. Nancy saw an event that was to stay in her memory forever.

She later spoke about it:

"The stormtroopers had tied the Jewish people up to massive wheels. They were rolling the wheels along, and the stormtroopers were whipping the Jews. I stood there and thought, I don't know what I'll do about it, but if I can do anything one day, I'll do it. And I always had that picture in my mind, all through the war."

6. The French Resistance

Nancy Wake remembered what she had seen in Austria. Henri and Nancy decided to support the French Resistance. Henri was a rich businessman. Nancy had an ability to travel in a way that few others could. She obtained false papers that allowed her to stay in the southern French-controlled zone and work.

During this time, Nancy made good connections and socialised with many people. Nancy and her husband were actively involved in the Resistance. They were involved with the beginning of the Resistance movement.

They smuggled messages and food to underground groups in southern France. She also bought an ambulance and would drive refugees to safety, fleeing the German advance.

By 1942, the Gestapo had started to become aware of an unidentified agent that was proving to be "a thorn in their side". The Gestapo wanted to catch the *White Mouse*, and listed her as number one on their most wanted list, offering a five million franc reward.

Nancy was doing a lot to help the Resistance and causing the Germans to be tied up looking for her.

The Gestapo were desperate to catch the *White Mouse*. Nancy Wake heard about their plans and escaped to England. She joined a special training unit called the French Section of the British Special Operations Executive (SOE). At this time, she was trained by the British to become a spy. She learnt how to parachute out of a plane, how to communicate and send coded reports, and learnt self-defence.

After her spy training, Nancy parachuted back into France. When she returned to France she carried weapons for Resistance fighters.

She also helped prepare the Resistance fighters for the famous D-Day landings. These preparations included giving leadership to 7,500 Resistance fighters who helped support the D-Day battle.

7. The White Mouse

Nancy Wake with her husband Henri became active in the Resistance movement saving thousands of Allied lives. How did they do this?

When Allied fighters escaped from the Germans, the French Resistance would feed them and protect them. They would show them the best paths to take to escape from France into neutral Spain. They would evade being captured by the Germans. The Resistance fighters would show them safe paths to travel to Spain.

Nancy and Henri were involved with smashing German installations. The Germans were desperate to capture the *White Mouse*.

In 1943, when the Germans became more aware of her activities, she escaped to Spain and continued her journey to Britain. She travelled on the same escape path as many of the Allied soldiers had done.

The *White Mouse* escaped again. Sadly, her husband Henri was captured and executed.

8. Did the Germans Find the *White Mouse*?

As the war continued, Nancy returned to France to support the Resistance. She parachuted back into France to help the French Resistance.

Henri Tardivat, one of her comrades, later said:

"She is the most feminine woman I know, until the fighting starts. Then she is like five men."

Nancy Wake put herself in the thick of the action. And yet the Gestapo never discovered who she was.

In 1944, the French Resistance reported that "the supply drops were threatened by the destruction of the radio coders."

These supply drops were ammunition, food, and information that were supplied to the French Resistance to help the Allies. However, back in 1944 the communications were not as good as what we have today.

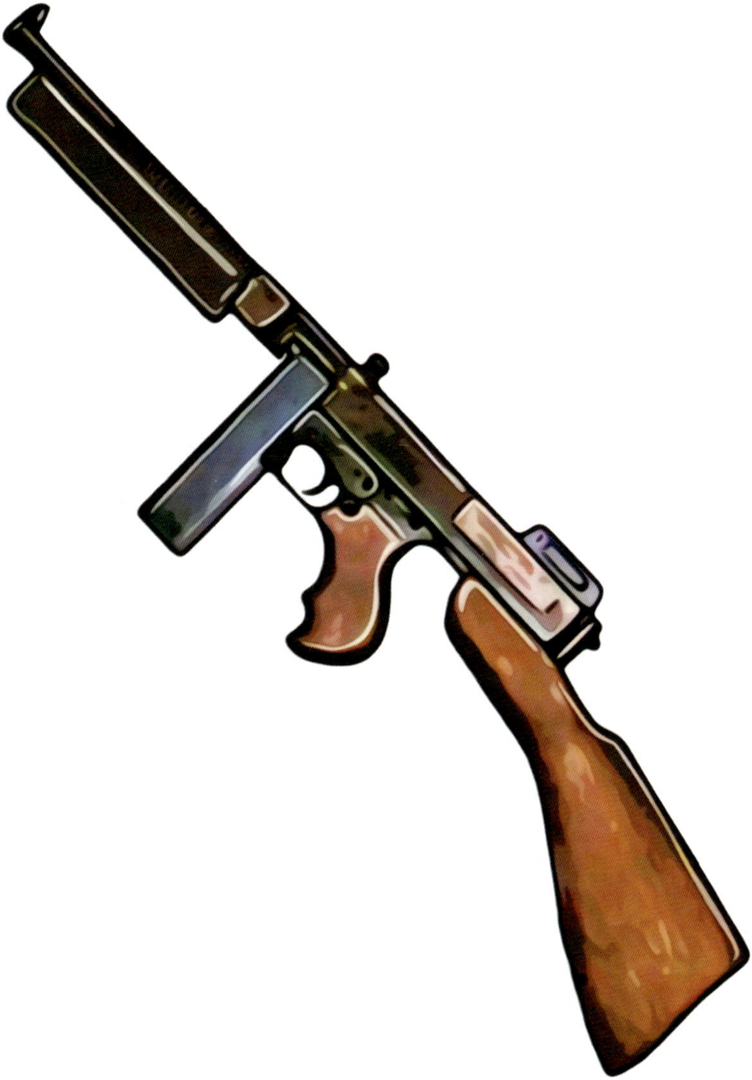

When the French Resistance and the British army talked, they used coders. These coders used a language that the Germans could not understand. Only the communications people trained for it could translate the codes.

When the radio coders had been destroyed, Nancy Wake knew that she had to get the message about the supply drops to the Allies.

Nancy Wake decided to take the important message to headquarters herself. She embarked on a marathon bicycle ride. She rode five hundred kilometres on her bike to get the message to headquarters.

She succeeded in completing the five-hundred-kilometre bicycle ride. Nancy passed the message to headquarters. She crossed several German check points and completed the ride in seventy-two hours. Nancy Wake took the job because she felt that, as a woman, she had more chance of passing through the checkpoints. She succeeded in delivering the message!

36

9. The War Ends

After the war, Nancy Wake received numerous international honours. Nancy is also regarded as a heroine in France, which decorated her with its highest military honour, the *Legion d'Honneur*, as well as three *Croix de Guerre* and a *French Resistance* Medal. She was also awarded Britain's *George Medal,* the US *Medal of Freedom*, and she was made a *Companion of the Order of Australia* in 2004.

As for her home country, despite being recommended for medals by the RSL, she only received her Australian award a long time after receiving the awards from Britain and France.

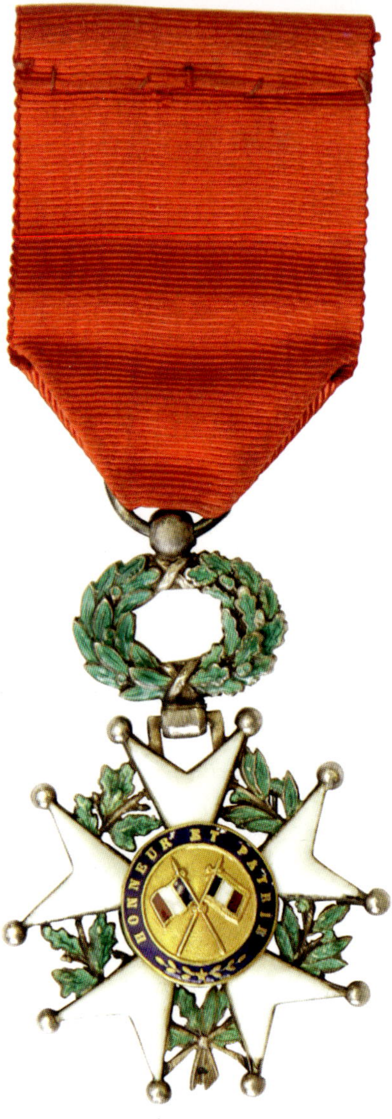
HONNEUR ET PATRIE

The Companion of the Order Of Australia read as follows, *"War hero: The award recognises the significant contribution and commitment of Nancy Wake, stemming from her outstanding actions in wartime, in encouraging community appreciation and understanding of the past sacrifices made by Australian men and women in times of conflict, and to a lasting legacy of peace."*

Nancy had no children but at her award ceremony she had a message for young Australians.

"To honour your mother and father, your family, to be truthful.... don't steal or get mixed up with drugs and things like that."

"There's no point in doing anything like that. All this behaviour doesn't mean you can't have fun."

"In fact, you can have more fun because the world is safer."

Nancy Wake was independent and resourceful from a young age.

She was the Allies' most decorated World War Two servicewoman and is revered in France as a national hero for her Resistance work and bravery.

In 1960, Nancy Wake returned to Australia. She wrote her story and called it, *The White Mouse*. She was also interested in politics, and stood for election in 1966 but failed to win her seat.

In 2001, she returned to England to live out her days with the express wish that her ashes be scattered over France after she died.

Nancy died in London in 2011, at the age of 98. What an amazing life and person!

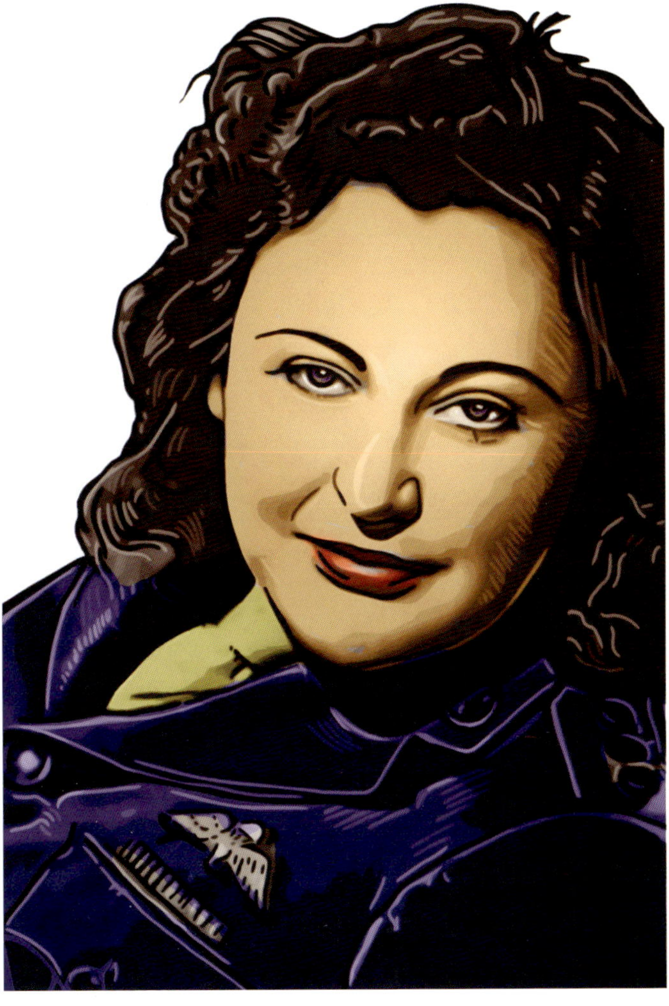

Word Bank

France	behaviour
Australia	remembered
Resistance	preparation
politics	responsibility
interested	journalist
scattered	refugees
servicewomen	sacrifices
parachute	Gestapo
decorated	inheritance